Lavinia J Lawrence

Euthanasia

And Other Poems

Lavinia J Lawrence

Euthanasia
And Other Poems

ISBN/EAN: 9783744760935

Printed in Europe, USA, Canada, Australia, Japan

Cover: Foto ©Thomas Meinert / pixelio.de

More available books at **www.hansebooks.com**

EUTHANASIA

AND

OTHER POEMS.

BY

LAVINIA J. LAWRENCE.

PHILADELPHIA :
TURNER & CO.,
NO. 808 CHESTNUT STREET.

VERNON & COOPER, Steam Power Book and Job Printers, Media, Pa.

TABLE OF CONTENTS.

TO MY DEAR AUNT,

Jane L. Simmons,

This volume is affectionately inscribed.

EUTHANASIA.

GENTLY, gently close the casement,
   'Gainst the tide of wind and storm,
That the midnight air intrusive
   May not chill the wasting form.
Closer draw the warmest mantle
   'Round the frame in deep decay,
Where the life-blood slowly ebbing
   Leaves its domain wan as clay.

But no warmth will come, no feeling
   To the surface still and cold,
Human efforts unavailing
   Mark the truth too plainly told.
Death will come, disease will conquer,
   Though the spirit may rebel,

And the vital spark will vanish,
  How or when, one scarce can tell.

She had been, that noble image
  Of God's pure creative power,
Weeks and months in hope delusive,
  Warding off the dying hour.
Time was when the brightest · talents
  Beamed forth from those speaking eyes,
When the world applauded wisdom
  That inspired truth implies.

When with voice and pen contending
· For humanity's just claims,
'Twas her spirit thrilled responsive,
  To the triumphs justice gains.
But Consumption claims its victim,
  And the hectic flush appeared,—
Friends have watched and still are watching
  O'er the form that love endeared.

Scarce three months since angel voices
  Called her widowed mother home,
Save the golden chain of friendship,
  Was the sufferer left alone.
There she lies—the youthful maiden,
  Death's cold damp is gathering now,
Night without—within the brightness
  That illumes the Christian's brow!

Pain—no pain intrudes ; but calmly,
  With no heavy labored breath,
Sinks the soul to rest : revealing
  But a passive, easy death.
Silently approach, unbeliever,
  Tremble for the promised boon,
God is here—repent, acknowledge,
  Lest thy summons come too soon.

Lo! a light is gently breaking
  O'er the placid, dying face,
Listen ! as angelic voices

Whisper of God's power and grace.

Hark! in gentle, rippling murmurs,

   She proclaims that Heaven is won:

"Music, oh, delightful music,—

   "Mother—dear—I come!—I come!

Gone! the golden gates are opened,

   To admit an angel there,

And the life that knew no shadow,

   Now fulfills the Christian's prayer.

Gone! oh, Death, what solemn warnings,

   Hast thou unto mortals given—

What a world of priceless treasures,

   Earth has yielded unto Heaven!

THOUGHTS ON SPRING.

WINTER departs—in classic beauty set,

    Nature's fresh garlands crown the brow of day,

Spring time returns without one sad regret,

    The icy monarch yields his wonted sway.

Soft notes of sylvan music fill the air,

    Unbounded power the mountain zephyrs claim,

The songster's lay re-echoes everywhere,

    And Draba Verna decks the sandy plain.

All that is lovely is contained within

The glorious advent of etherial Spring.

No sophistry on vernal breezes borne,

    To lead the weary wanderer astray,

No thickening vapors dim the cloudless morn—

    Remnants of Winter's reign are swept away.

The mellow tint of yonder azure sky,

  The robin perched upon the lattice bower,

Warbling in silver notes' sweet lullaby,

  Bring mirth and gladness to the passing hour.

From rippling stream, from meadow and from brake,

Comes the soft summons, nature awake! awake!

Responsive springs the clover from the sod,

  The moss-grown rocks a verdant tint display,

Each blade of grass gives homage unto God,

  For nature's works admit of no delay.

Mild waves of ether floating noiselessly,

  Are redolent with incense-breathing flowers,

Lifting their modest forms from marshy lea,

  Regaled by sunbeams and by tepid showers.

Thus while successive seasons onward roll,

Are there not greater changes of the soul?

Oh, wanderer, searching for the inward light,

  Canst thou not reap a harvest of ideas

From nature's meek obedience—conquering strife—

To lift the burden of advancing years?
Art thou so blind, creative wisdom fails
   To make impression on thy sordid mind?
Art thou so deaf, that in refreshing gales,
   And warbling brooks, no comfort thou canst
     find?
If so, what subtle power of inward strife
Obscures with clouds the day-star of thy life.

Perhaps, in one brief, fleeting season, thou
   Hast offered treasures at thy country's shrine,
And grief's dark pall has settled on thy brow,—
   Check not the tear—such weeping is sublime!
Oh, may religion through life's mazes lead
   Thy spirit rejoicing to the promised goal,
Not by the force of outward prayer or creed,
   But the pure inward current of the soul.
Then to the breezes all life's trials fling,
Go forth stout-hearted with the early Spring.

I would not martyr graves, sunk and time-worn,

Be e'er forgot in Spring's effulgent bliss,
But sound the requiem—let the stranger's form
Tread gently, gently ; hallowed soil is this.
'Mid loyal graves the deep-dyed traitor cowers,
And gathering incense fills the air around,
While nature in profusion scatters flowers,
With growing verdure decks the sacred mound.
Above them let the star-gemmed banner wave,
No mausoleum need the fallen brave!

Relentless Winter! fare thee well, no more
Dark gathering tempests haunt the sailor's brain,
A holy calm extends from shore to shore,
O'er earth's green surface as across the main.
And as the waters of contending strife,
Receding leave the Nation purified,
Living a brighter, truer, nobler life,
The olive branch of peace spread far and wide ;
Thus as we cease relentless war to mourn,
In peace and joy another Spring is born!

LINES DEDICATED TO "GIDEONS' BAND," 124TH REGIMENT, P. V.,

SEPTEMBER 5TH, 1862.

ON, soldiers, on! let your watchword ever be
"The home of the brave, the land of the free!"
Tossed o'er the waters of war's crimson tide,
Traitors may boast and your courage deride,
Yet above all, through the unequal strife,
Rises the triumpet–call, "God and the Right!"
While the swift meteors of thought may reveal
Seasons of doubt 'midst the glittering steel;
Yet as the flashes of lightning appear,
Fade o'er the horizon gloomy and drear,
Thus the brief moments of hopeless despair
Vanish for aye! 'midst the battle's red glare.
On, soldiers, on! like the Spartans of old,

15

Rush to the rescue determined and bold!

Though the strong battlements yield to the foe,

Wisdom and bravery may weaken the blow.

For as the Israelites fled in dismay,

Faith in the Savior yet opened the way.

Faith in Jehovah the waters divide,

Our brave "Israelites" pass o'er the tide.

Through the fierce conflict the noble and brave,

May irresistible destiny save.

Oh! may the breezes still faithful and true,

Waft o'er the Northern hills blessings to you,

Blessings from anxious hearts sad and forlorn,

Prayers that the laurels of glory adorn.

Manhood's strong effort the nation to save,

From that oblivion which follows the grave.

On, soldiers, on! yield not to the foe,

Though unpropitious the breezes may blow;

Trustful reliance on God and the Right,

Softens the spirit of discord and strife.

When by unchanging faith freedom is won,

When the bright lustre of liberty's sun,

Dims the blind sophism oppression may raise,

Send forth the anthems of prayer and of praise.

Yet will our banner triumphantly wave,

History record the acts of the brave ;

Then may the tidings descend through the land,

" Bravest of the brave" was "Gideon's Band."

THE SEASONS.

As the orb of day reflecting the celestial beams
of light,
Clothes the world with life and gladness, pictures
heaven to our sight ;
As the modest wayside flower wafts its incense
on the air,
Cheers the traveller's lonely passage, soothes his
senses free from care ;
So the harbinger of beauty, followed by her
fairy train,
Brightening many clouds of sorrow, gentle Spring
returns again.
Azure sky and verdant meadows, leafy woods and
budding flowers,

18

Glitter brightly through the sunshine that is
dimmed by morning showers.

So the balmy zephyrs moving in their silent
onward way,

Call the birds from warmer regions, wake to life
the songsters gay.

As we trace life's destined passage from the cradle
to the bier,

May we not compare youth's beauty to the
Spring-time of the year.

How the child, like spring's fair flowers roving in
his childish glee,

How the bud of promise opens, bursting forth
half timidly.

But not long the Great Jehovah deemed that
Spring should reign supreme,

Summer dawns in all her glory, and "a change
comes o'er my dream."

How a thousand memories cluster 'round the
farmer's busy brain,

As he views his store increasing, gleans the
    bright and golden grain.

Thus how beautiful the season that completes the
    works of Spring,

As all animated nature aid the praise of God
    to sing.

So with human life—for Summer representing
    manhood's prime,

When we look with hope increasing down the
    misty vale of Time,

Little dreaming that the future, Autumn or de-
    cline of life,

Soon may change our happy prospects, sear our
    hearts with mortal strife.

All our aspirations rosy, bearing impress half
    divine,

We forget the soul is kneeling to a mortal
    human shrine.

Autumn comes—and slowly, surely Summer's works
    decline, decay,

For the woods, the vales, the mountains lay their

emerald robes away.

As the herbage, yellow-tinted, rustling borne upon the breeze,

Floats upon the crystal waters, and among the forest trees.

For our Heavenly Father ordered that the forests decked with green,

Should be stripped of Summer's foliage, represent another scene.

Thus the buoyancy of manhood, thus does human life decline,

Age and adverse winds of fortune change the current of the mind.

Winter next, with hasty footstep, with a brow of hope bereft,

Gathers up with mournful visage, all the remnants that are left.

How the birds seek warmer regions soaring proudly through the sky,

How each leaf and tendril drooping, in their beauty sicken, die.

Nature dons her wintry garments, change is
marked upon her form,

As the snow-flakes chase each other in the fury
of the storm.

Just so transient man's existence, life that's
blooming bright to-day,

Ere to-morrow's sun has risen, leaves its domain
wan as clay.

Wonderful, Almighty Father, are these earthly
works of Thine,

Making closer the alliance of the simple and
sublime.

Death may still the trembling accents, as the
spirit roams above,

Yet the wild winds 'midst our mourning gently
whisper "God is love!"

THE AMERICAN FLAG.

WAVE ON! thou emblem of the free,
 A nation owns thy power divine,
Life was not lost in vain for thee,
 For yet thy starry jewels shine.
Responding to the trumpet's sound,
 Thousands rush forward to defend,
Nobly and well they gather 'round
 That honored flag which traitors rend.

Wave on! in memory of the brave,
 The youthful heart beats warm and high,
The noble spirit flies to save—
 To strike the blow, to do or die.
The organ's mystic notes proclaim
 The soul's devotion unto thee,

And every voice with one acclaim,
    Joins in the chorus of the free.

Wave on! our cause is just and right,
    Though wrong may triumph for a time,
Though dreary clouds may dim the sight,
    The dawn of light will be sublime.
That golden heritage of love
    Bequeathed by patriots of yore,
That glorious tribute from above,
    Calls us to arms, to speed the war.

Wave on! oppression's hand has swayed
    The iron rod, alas! too long,
And Freedom though oppressed, obeyed,
    But now she combats with the wrong.
Though great the sacrifice may be,
    Though brave and noble men may fall,
Yet waves the banner of the free,
    Freedom will triumph over all.

Wave on! for God is with the right,
    Let the brave spirit watch and pray,
He will dispel the clouds of night,
    Give to the just eternal day.

Beneath the beams of freedom's sun,
    Oppression finds an early grave,
For freedom's victory will be won,
    Our honored flag forever wave!

THE AFRICAN PILOT.

MAY we not, whose minds are centered on
the dark eventful days,

Which have passed in quick succession 'neath the
sunlight's fading rays,

Trace the yet unwritten history of the deeds of
valor won

By a noble-hearted hero, Africa's untutored son.

Anchored in a southern harbor, the majestic
" Planter " lay,

As her dark-skinned pilot waited breathlessly for
dawn of day.

As the Orient light was breaking o'er the dark
imprisoned sky,

Nature waking from her reverie, the Palmetto
floating high ;

Silently she left the harbor, while the rebel guns
were mute,

For the brave and skillful pilot boldly gave the
wild salute.

Onward past the forts she glided, softly o'er the
dark blue sea,

Nearer and still nearer wending to the shore of
liberty.

Past the rebel forts—how quickly was the white
flag hoisted high,

Till its white folds calmly waving seemed to
reach the azure sky.

And a prayer of mute thanksgiving rose above
that grateful crew,

Aye! a thousand times more touching and a
thousand times more true,

Than the empty-hearted blessings which so oft
ascend above,

Falling without thought or purpose on the throne
of heavenly love.

Instinct taught thee, noble pilot, and the deed
  was bravely done ;

It is thine to wear unblushing all the laurels
  richly won.

It is thine when evening shadows usher in the
  star-gemmed night,

Or at dawn of day reflecting beams of clear and
  lucid light,

To enjoy the boon of freedom to thy injured
  race denied.

Still the land is draped in mourning, still flows
  on the crimson tide,

For an unseen spirit reigneth to whose dictates
  all must bow,

And an unseen hand is weaving garlands for the
  captive's brow.

After months of anxious waiting, years of unrequited toil,

The expanding bud of promise crushed beneath
  the serpent's coil ;

Thou hast gained the full fruition in thy manhood's early prime,
As the glorious light of freedom dawns in beauty
  half divine.
There are those whose barks are floating on life's
  dark and stormy sea,
Tossed upon the billowy waters, who will shape
  our destiny.
Aye! too true—the storm is raging fiercely o'er
  the white man's home,
But a great mysterious Being hears the captive's
  pleading tone,
And if man is blind to duty, to the still small
  voice within,
We may place this land's redemption 'midst the
  things which might have been.

CAN we not as gliding onward,

Down the mazy path of Time,

By the souls who have departed

To that "undiscovered clime,"

Learn a task of mild submission,

To the ills that may betide,

Drink from out the cup of wisdom

By a spirit sanctified.

Thus where nature clothed in beauty,

Charms the senses, cheers the day,

Where the happy, chirping songster

Chaunts his solemn evening's lay ;

There beside the murmuring streamlet,

Where the air is pure and mild,

30

Free from all the world's contagion ;

Roved Von Humboldt as a child.

Born into this world of Science,

Thou wast still the guiding star,

Spreading thy immortal knowledge

O'er the selfish world afar.

Thou hast crossed the broad Atlantic,

Stemmed the current of Life's tide,

Thou in foreign lands hast wandered,

O'er the rugged mountain's side.

While ascending Chimborazo,

Sick at heart and tempest tossed,

'Mid the hail and drifting snow–storm,

'Mid the cold and bleaching frost,

Suddenly the vapor parted,

Thus in vain thou didst not roam,

In the distance rose before thee,

Chimborazo's snow–capped dome.

Nearer and still nearer wending,

Farther from the earth below,

But, alas! when Hope is strongest,

Oft appears the cup of woe ;

For thy joyous expectation

Soon to stand upon the dome,

Vanished as a fearful chasm

Bade thee not to longer roam.

Even age did not diminish,

Change the current of thy mind,

Through the frosts of many winters,

Thou wast gentle, loving, kind.

As the foe of stern oppression,

As the friend of Truth and Right,

Thou hast found the narrow passage

Leading to Eternal Life.

Brave old man! now fairy music

Lulls thy weary soul to rest,

With a diadem of glory,

Golden laurels thou art blest,

And thy "Kosmos," full of beauty.

Charms the world with power divine.

Leads the thoughts from airy visions,

From the simple to sublime.

As a lamp when dimly burning

Did thy new existence dawn,

Fainter and still fainter gleaming,

'Till the spark of life was gone.

Then thy spirit wafted homeward,

Borne unto that happy land,

While a smile of recognition

Shone around the angel band.

GATHERED 'round the blazing embers,

When the Winter day is o'er, ·

Sit our aged sires relating

Deed of noble sons of yore.

How they fought and won the victory—

Wading through a crimson sea,

How they fought and how they conquered,

For a land of Liberty.

While the child and youthful maiden,

Quick to catch the thrilling sound,

Quick to bless the names of heroes

Who are lain beneath the mound,

Cluster near with mind attentive,

As the grey yarn they transform

34

From a thread of various texture,

To grey stockings nice and warm.

Swiftly fly the knitting needles,

As the shrill wind whistles low,

While grandmother in the corner,

Pictures scenes of "long·ago."

How the "girls" of seventy–six—

"Ladies" were unknown then—

Worked from mourn till eve incessant,

For the patriotic men.

"Little dreamed they when the British

Fled before brave Washington,

That alas! dark clouds would gather

In the year of sixty–one.

Yet how deeply erred our fathers,

In our country's early life,

Fostering here oppression's power,

Source of all our mortal strife!"

" But, my dear," unto the youngest

   Of that happy knitting band,

" You may live to see triumphant,

   See redeemed our native land.

So knit on ; the weary soldier

   Through the fierce and raging storm,

Will not fail to bless the donor

   Of grey stockings nice and warm."

As she ceased the blazing embers

   Having lost their vital power,

While the clock as if impatient

   Tolled the solemn midnight hour ;

One by one the band of knitters

   Whispered soft the fond "good-night."

Many a prayer and many a blessing,

   For the brave who fought for right.

AN APPEAL.

" Theirs was the singular fortune to go to their first
battle under a cloud of reproach, though blameless,
and to return from it victorious, to the punishment re-
served for the gravest military offences."—*Mrs. Fre-
mont's "Story of the Guard."*

CZAR of the North, the South, the East and
 West!

Whose power contending factions make supreme,

Let not the deeds of honest merit rest,

 Naught but the bright illusion of a dream.

Ruler of State! the true and brave demand

 Some recompense that they alone may claim,

Some confirmation spread throughout the land,

 That o'er the nation Truth and Justice reign.

37

Thou who Ambition's feeble race hast run,

    Send forth those words of cheer the troopers

    crave,

Let not the wisdom human valor won,

    Sink to the dark oblivion of the grave!

Then may the world as ceaseless ages roll,

    In retrospection, bless thy honored name,

As one who bravely reached the promised goal!

    And Heaven-directed trod the path of fame!

And ye now clothed with Legislative power,

    Whose voices bold through Senate halls have

    rung,

As duty prompts improve the passing hour,

    While time records the deeds of justice done.

Look on the blood-stained valleys of the West!

    Mute witnesses of bravery grand but rare,

How many blossoms faded on her breast,

    How many cherished hopes are buried there!

None but that unseen power, at whose command
  The boon of Freedom may be lost or won,
Can know the trials of that patriot band,
  From conquest borne, "unhonored and unsung."

Yet will impartial history justly trace
  Those scenes eclipsed by naught that virtue
    claims,
Those deeds that time alone cannot efface,
  More brilliant still the gallant Guard remains.

To those who dyed the Western hills with gore,
  A haven theirs of life, and hope, and song,
But for the mortal, we with faith implore
  A day of promise for a night of wrong!

JOSEPHINE, EMPRESS OF FRANCE.

A S we trace the simple record, mark the progress of the great,

In the march of human wisdom note the hero's
life and fate;

How unto the mental vision, reverence for the
true and brave

Rises like the ocean's current, swells with each
succeeding wave.

On that isle renowned for beauty, verdant valleys,
warm her plains,

Where the sea-breeze cools her homesteads, nature paints her mountain chains;

Martinique her crystal fountains, charming with a
potent power,

40

Forests yielding health and beauty, fascinate each
　　passing hour ;
Josephine, the loved, the cherished, where con-
　　tentment reigned supreme,
Opened first her eyes to glory, smiled on nature's
　　lovely scene.
As the years of childhood flitted, child of nature,
　　pure and good,
Strengthened by thy forest rambles, blossomed
　　into womanhood.
The old Sibyl's strange prediction, thou as Queen
　　of France would reign,
Wield the rod of truth and justice o'er the
　　mazy path of fame ;
Fell upon thy youthful spirit, lit with purity and
　　love,
As a ray of worthless wisdom, not a message
　　from above.
Years rolled on : that simple lesson taught by a
　　magician's art,

Fills thy soul with truth undoubting, claims a
    sanctum in thy heart.

Crowned within the lordly presence as Napoleon's
    queenly bride,

Yet retaining truth and virtue conquered not by
    human pride.

But those halcyon months of pleasure soon, alas,
    must disappear,

Be replaced by days of sadness, nights of sorrow
    long and drear.

But the heart that could so rudely, for ambition
    slumbering there,

Break the tendrils of affection, change thy hopes
    to mute despair,

Must possess an unknown power, hard as ada-
    mant must be,

Thus to turn his thoughts like magic, far away
    from love and thee.

Child of Destiny! thy answer to Napoleon's stern
    command,

Yet demands a passing tribute from some poet's

skillful hand.

Pointing to a star of promise in the firmament
above ;

" See ! that star of promise brightens as it shines
upon our love ;

" It is mine—proclaiming power, certain victory to
thee,

" If I share the joys and sorrows that will mark
thy destiny.

" Leave me—and thy· honors fading on ambition's
gilded throne,

" As that star of promise fadeth, thou wilt die
obscure, unknown.

" Yield this phantom ! search for wisdom in the
vales of happy France,

" Sweet retirement soon will banish all these
visions from thy glance."

As these words, this gentle counsel seemed to
check the Emperor's frown,

Yet the voice of France did conquer—honor
yielded to renown.

With that stern, resistless power that had marked
    his former years,

Did Napoleon sign the death–warrant of thy
    cherished hopes and fears.

Thus thy spirit,, noble woman, by the storms of
    life was driven,

As thy bark moved gently onward to a peaceful
    rest in Heaven.

It is not the Kings, the Princes, those the world
    style noble birth,   ·

Who alone proclaim thy virtue, mourning for de-
    parted worth ;

But the poor, the weak, the lowly, aid the com-
    mon human tide,

Heaven now embalms thy image with the love
    that Earth denied.   ,

THE VOLUNTEER.

ACROSS the wide expanse of nature's scene,
  The trumpet-call re-echoed soft and clear,
O'er Northern hill with firm determined mien,
  And soul responding, walked the volunteer.

The last sweet accents of a mother's love,
  A father's and a sister's last farewell,
The gentle words of faith in Heaven above,
  The silent tear, which though forbidden fell;

Marked the deep conflict of the soul within,
  And left their impress on his manly heart,
That years of absence through this vale of sin,
  Leave unimpaired what faith and love impart.

The moon–lit sky, the clear and frosty air,
  The jeweled firmament above revealed
Unto his saddened spirit, rest is there,
  Though storm–clouds oft those golden orbs
    concealed.

Into the guarded tent the warrior came,
  While restless sleepers all around him lay,
Their anxious looks in fitting words proclaim,
  The foe's expected march at dawn of day.

The countersign by manly lips was given,
  In easy slumber sank the weary band,
While memory pictured scenes—an earthly heaven,
  When peace triumphant dawns upon the land!

Aye! who may know what fitful visions break
  The peaceful slumber of the warrior brave?
Aye! who may know what sweet illusions wake
  The tender blessings home so freely gave?

As tints of grey proclaim the early morn,
  The eastern sky in silver jewels set,
And bugle–notes by trembling zephyrs borne,
  The warrior clasps his trusty bayonet.

Next we behold him on the battle–field,
  His comrades faltering 'neath the cruel steel,
But, "courage! courage! boys, the foe must
      yield!"
  Rose from those manly lips in firm appeal.

Like magic formed the broken ranks again,
  With one bold charge the battle–field was won!
But, oh, America! thy victory then
  Lost half its worth—when fell thy noblest son.

His comrades bore him from the gory scene,
  And wept in silence o'er that form so dear,
While wayward fancy—sweet delusion's dream,
  Cheered the last moments of the volunteer.

Oh, there are those whose noble instincts bear

Divine impression language fails to paint,

While every impulse—every feeble prayer,

Breathe the pure feelings of the martyr saint !

At morn in triumph rose the golden sun,

As conquest crowned with blessings freedom's
race,

At eve the grave's stern victory was won,

As sank the mortal frame in death's embrace.

L I N E S.

Suggested by the death of William P. Lawrence, who departed this life, February 16th, 1862.

" Blessed are the dead who die in the Lord."

As the golden tint of sunset mantling o'er the
  distant west,

Fades before the march of evening o'er the
  ocean's jewelled breast,

And the beauty of the landscape tinted with
  celestial dye,

Sinks beneath the darkened vision as the evening
  hour draws nigh,

Thus the forms we love and cherish, blighted by
  the frosts of time,

Seek a home among the blessed, in that happier,
  holier clime.

Aye, another tie is broken—tears have flowed in
  lava tide,

Yet how vain the words thus spoken o'er a spirit
sanctified.

Thought, deep thought was firmly centered in thy
ever tranquil mind,

To a higher field of labor in response thy soul
inclined.

When the mind was weak and feeble, reason
tottered on her throne,

Yet thy spirit did not wander through the path
of life alone.

For that all–sustaining wisdom which the Christian soul may see,

An undying, never–changing faith in immortality

Buoyed thee up beyond the changes that contending life may yield,

Marked a noble sphere of action on a broad ex-
pansive field.

To this world of pain and pleasure, to this ever-
changing clime,

Would we call thee back from glory, call thee
from that home divine?

No! oh no! though ties are severed and the
trembling feet may stray,

Yet a truer life is dawning on the resurrection
day.

Angel hands now weave the garlands which adorn
thy placid brow,

And the friends who knew and loved thee feel
thy heavenly presence now,

Making closer the connection. of the living and
the dead,

Though in lonely contemplation the unconscious
tears are shed.

But a little while we linger, drinking of the
treasured love,

For the vital spark is weaker as we near the
heavenly shore. .

When the "angel bridegroom" cometh as a sweet
release from sin,

May our lamps be trimmed and burning, as we
feel that thine has been.

AN INCIDENT OF THE NEW YORK
RIOT.

" Mother they may kill the body but they cannot
touch the soul ! "

Peaceful o'er the placid waters rose the radiant
summer's sun,

Loyal voices shouted anthems o'er the conquest
bravely won.

For the walls of Vicksburg yielded to the Union
shot and shell,

While Port Hudson trembling waited but a clearer
tale to tell.

Yet, alas ! day's golden image scarce had left its
impress there,

When above a Northern city rose the sounds of
wild despair.

52

Fiends and demons yet unnumbered rallied forth
   in bold array,

Deeds of darkness, scenes of carnage marked the
   traitors' onward way.

Blind to feeling, deaf to mercy, who may judge
   the depth of crime ;

None but God may know the misery traced upon
   the book of Time.

'Tis enough that sinking manhood, with consumption's hectic glow,

Fell a prey to ruffian anger—sank beneath a
   coward's blow.

Brutish force conveyed the "loved one" from that
   widowed mother's side,

While her groans of mortal anguish echoed back
   intensified.

But the God of races lifted up the mantle of
   despair,

And revealed the crown of glory that her dying
   son would wear.

While upon that lucid countenance sin had left
   no bitter trace,

But 'a look of earnest meaning lit the dying
   hero's face.

Whispering words of cheer and comfort as he
   neared the promised goal,

"Mother, they may kill the body, but they cannot touch the soul."

What a world of earnest meaning do these words
   of faith convey,

As religion sheds its lustre brilliant as the light
   of day.

What a stern rebuke to madness, could the faith-
   less soul believe,

Ages of self–abnegation, years of prayer can scarce
   retrieve.

Aye! humanity may envy Abraham Franklin's
   peaceful grave,

While the hearts of unborn millions will his
   heavenly advent crave.

And those simple words of feeling bid the waves
of thought to roll,

" Mother they may kill the body, but they cannot touch the soul."

Vainly may we search in history what the bar-
barous ages tell,

St. Batholomew's dark record scarcely seems a
parallel.

Yet the day of triple vengeance hastens forth
on nimble wing,

And the time of true repentance proves the fact
that God is King.

But those foes to reigning justice never can the
past restore,

Though that widowed mother's image haunts their
days forevermore.

As a monument of glory faithfully these words
enroll,

" Mother, they may kill the body, but they cannot touch the soul !"

STANZAS,

I SAW thee when the joys of maidenhood,

　　Held spell–bound every thought of grief and
　　　pain ;

Upon thy brow the virgin's wreathlet stood,

　　Upon thy soul temptation left no stain.

While inspiration lit thy inner shrine,

　　Illuming o'er the secret wells of thought,

The Poet's talent, though not wholly thine,

　　With potent spell a nobler spirit wrought.

We met as only friends congenial meet,

　　Upon the threshold of unbounded love,

56

And drank with rapture from the fountain deep,
The choicest blessing issuing from above.

While thou, the senior—both with purpose brave,
With mutual thoughts and aspirations high,
We bounded lightly o'er life's billowy wave—
Years of communion passing swiftly by.

One phase in life I may not yet reveal,
'Tis held as sacred as the stars above!
Aye, sad indeed those hearts that blindly reel,
Clasping the phantom—unrequited love.

Time passed: I met thee on thy bridal eve,
Affection's wreath adorned thy placid brow,
While tender hands the verdant garlands wreathe,
Thou, ever faithful, spoke the marriage vow.

Strange! while the hearts of mortals throb with
joy,

A doubtful shadow flits across the brain,
Lest future prospects prove a base alloy,
Too feeble to support the trembling frame.

Lest woman's love, so nobly, truly given,
Be fostered only to be rudely spurned,
While his dominion is her earthly Heaven,
His smiles the Paradise to which she turned.

Again I saw thee in thy happiest hours,
Parental smiles fell o'er thy infant boy,
For destiny has strewn thy path with flowers,
And each pulsation seems a world of joy.

I leave thee here ; life's golden wreath is thine !
May Heaven e'er smile so lovingly on thee !
And may the choicest gifts of hoary Time,
Gladden thy pathway o'er life's troubled sea !

THE HERO OF NEW ORLEANS.

HAIL! noble Chief! fair fortune claims for thee,

   The richest crown artistic skill may form,

An emblem of that cherished liberty,

   Choice heritage to millions yet unborn!

Thy deeds immortal crowd the human gaze, .

And shine more brilliant through the darkening

   haze.

When o'er the Crescent City dimly shone

   The half extinguished sun of freedom's race,

From watching souls, in touching, piteous tone,

   Arose a prayer unto the throne of Grace,

That some bright spirit from the martial field,

Should clasp the wand oppression dared to wield!

The summons came : unflinchingly there stood

   The form of Butler ; 'midst the rebel bands—

Thou bid defiance to the multitude,

   Sent forth inflexibly thy just commands.

Aye, even so, the cannon's fearful roar,

Brought life and hope to that unhappy shore !

Yet prejudice, the scorn of future time,

   Still bade thee with a lenient hand control,

And sway the sceptre in that southern clime,

   With all the impulse of a generous soul.

But soon the die was cast—the dawn of day—

When Mumford tore the starry flag away !

Thy soul, indignant, laid the traitor low,

   Threw off the garb of lenity and love !

Flung to the breeze the ensign of the foe,

   Obedient to the stern command above !

Soon rampant Treason sunk his hydra head,

While soon the rod of Justice ruled instead !

And loyalty, whatever hue the skin,

   Obtained the patriot's reward from thee,

Exulting under thy protecting wing,

   Waved forth the glorious banner of the free!

No bright anticipations bathed in tears,

No blooming hopes dissolved in idle fears.

          •

Those halcyon months of unalloyed repose, ˙

   When manhood, felt the bonds of faith secure,

When Justice triumphed o'er disdainful foes,

   Shall live so long as memory may endure.

And priceless blessings for thee still remain,

Recalled when in the zenith of thy fame.

The freedman's heart pulsates in unison

   And thrills with gratitude and love to thee;

A foretaste of the life yet scarce begun,

   He sounds thy praises o'er the land and sea!

Of all brave deeds the patient eye may scan,

Brave-hearted Butler carries off the palm!

EVENING MEDITATIONS.

THE day is o'er ; the source of light and life,

Hath sunk to rest, and darkness shrouds the

earth,

Expressive silence 'neath the shades of night,

To things terrestial gives a holy birth.

I gaze delighted on the Heavens above,

'Till life seems sweet—one joyous round of love.

On yon pale crescent—yonder starry spheres,

The eye of faith in wayward fancy turns,

Bright memories quench the lava–tide of tears,

With greater lustre latent passion burns.

The languid spirits now uplifted high,

Drink from the treasures mirrored on the sky.

62

In vain my vision strives to pierce the veil
   That shrouds the future from our anxious gaze;
With each brave effort gloomy doubts assail,
   Darker and deeper grows the thickening haze.
'Till thought oppressed the spirit learns to trust,
Howe'er mysterious, all God's ways are just.

The moonbeams resting on the glassy lake
   Reflect the glory of a brighter world,
While passing clouds a fairer semblance take,
   Appear in all their magic power unfurled.
The distant planets now harmoniously
Revolve, in all their separate actions free.

What stream of lucid fire illumes the earth?
   Darting with lightning speed across the sky,
Wasting the splendor of a heavenly birth,
   Passing almost unnoticed quickly by?
The flashing meteor's still reflected glow
Beams on the sight—and all is bright below!

Celestial beauty charms with potent power,

As heavenward the thoughtful vision glides,

While peace and beauty rule the passing hour,

On one pale star the thankful eye abides.

Shining with grandeur now almost alone,

A beacon–light to guide the wanderer home.

What star is this? The bondman's hope and joy,

His only birthright 'neath the boundless skies

The oppressor's strong desire cannot destroy,

It twinkles on and every ill defies.

Emitting peaceful rays though distant far,

Shineth sublimely still the Northern star!

But why attempt description that must fail,

Why try, oh, God! to fathom the beyond?

To all excited fancy dares to hail,

Thy wonder–working mandates quick respond.

Enough thy bounteous blessings now to share,

Enough to know thy presence everywhere.

The midnight hour draws nigh. My senses feel

   A new, a strange delight; and hope is gay,

While faithful memory happy scenes reveal,

   Faith lends to idle fears the brightest ray.

To pleasing contemplation ever true,

To scenes of blissful reverie, adieu!

THE RESPONSE.

WRITTEN AFTER THE ELECTION OF GOV. CURTIN, 1863.

SACRED home of Penn and Freedom!

Anchored on the troubled sea,

Shall storm–clouds and surging billows

Gather o'er futurity?

Voices of the brave and daring

Blended with the just and true,

Shall they cease still all unheeded,

Mourned but by the loyal few?

Yet again the graves of heroes

Mantled with the verdant sod,

Do they not though dumb and speechless

Point to Justice and to God?

66

All the earnest hopes of manhood
  Mirrored on the azure sky,
While prophetic of the future,
  Shall they pass unnoticed by?

The response thrills through the nation,
  As electric sparks of fire!
Brightening every latent feeling,
  Tuning fresh the Poet's lyre!
Day advances—night is waning—
  While we find what justice claims,
Traced upon the scroll of honor,
  Fifteen thousand loyal names!

Would ye know the joyful throbbings
  All across the mighty main?
Ask of those whose dearest treasures
  Rest upon the battle plain.
For again our standard-bearer
  Clasps the trusty helm of State,

While the Ship with air defiant,
Bids the storm of war abate.

Saved : the nation's heart beats wildly,
As redeemed the Keystone stands !
While the subtle flame of treason,
Is obscured by loyal hands.
Saved : one shout of ardent feeling
Bursts upon the gladdened ear !
From unbroken ranks of freemen
Issues forth cheer after cheer !

While along the distant hillside,
Through the valleys rich and fair,
Float around soul–stirring anthems—
Treason yields to mute despair.
Faith and Hope again enkindled,
Stronger grow the mystic ties,
While the voice of Right and Power,
Rock–walled battlements defies !

Greater far this moral conquest,

 Binding with a potent power,

Crushing treason's lurking image,

 In this final crisis–hour,

Than those meteoric flashes

 Through the battle's blackening smoke,

Or the bayonet's reckless charges,

 Or the sabre's cruel stroke.

For with talismanic influence,

 Bursting forth in vital flame,

Deeds of conscience as of valor,

 Do a nation's homage claim.

Challenging the foes of freedom,

 With an impulse undenied,

Down the current of progression

 Sweeps humanity's broad tide!

A LAMENT.

DEAD! oh, ye mystic wanderers of night,

Stars of the first great magnitude above!

Where are the bright etherial realms of light?

Where hope and faith as guardian spirits rove?

Those midnight messengers of light still roam,

Twinkling in solemn grandeur. Aye! but now,

No marvellous sibyl's voice with magic tone,

Chases away the clouds upon my brow.

Dead! oh, brother, this world is drear and lone,

Clouded with waves of dark adversity,

Yet those who 'mid the din of battle roam,

Fear not the stern decrees of destiny.

70

Such was thy fate ; lost on the southern shore,

Virginia ! weep above thy fallen foe, ·

The golden scenes of blissful life are o'er,

While oracles of truth speak soft and low.

The silver wand of fame allured thee on,

Still is the life–pulse—calm the fevered brow,

Beneath the gorgeous beams of freedom's sun,

Thy star of promise set in grandeur now.

Dead! while the moon's pale beams serenely fall

Upon the bosom of the dark blue sea,

Thy voice no more re–echoes through the hall,

But all is veiled in one dread mystery.

Before thy vision faithful memory brings,

Those evanescent scenes of days gone by,

When at the dewy morn, the woodlark sings

His mournful requiem 'neath the azure sky.

9

But one is absent; one whose presence lent

    A charm unknown, save when the curtain fell

Upon my wounded heart with sorrow rent,

    Hope and joy faded with the funeral knell.

Oh, War! thou hast thy scenes of wild delight,

    When o'er the conqueror's brow the wreath of

        Bay

Twines its soft tendrils, joyful is the sight,

    A counterpart of Heaven's eternal day.

Again thy fearful moments of despair,

    The vanquished hero fills a martyr's grave,

As the sad anthems swell the mountain air,

    O'er one who died his cherished land to save.

Yet 'mid this world of dark and causeless strife,

    One precious boon to human mortals given,

One ray of hope—the guiding star of life,

    This sweet reflection, there is rest in Heaven!

THE SILVER LINING.

THE Ice-King reigned—the winter blast swept
  by,
Triumphantly the moonlight clear and bright,
Reflected all the glory of the sky,
  And crowned with garlands gay the brow of .
  night.

Without was peace. Within a maiden fair
  Knelt faithfully her lonely couch beside,
Breathing the silent accents of a prayer,
  To Him in whom all faith and hope abide.

                                        •

The impress of a sad and deep despair,
  Has left upon her brow a bitter trace,

Grief had displayed his sable mantle there,
And clouded over that once smiling face.

She loved : aye ! loved as all true women love,
The strongest passion of a virtuous heart ;
Sacred the thought—inspired from above
With all the zeal that angels may impart.

Not hers to know an unrequited flame,
And sigh o'er brightest virtues rudely spurned,
Not hers to weep—to mourn another's gain,
For mutually affection's fire burned.

He loved : the glance of pure affection stole .
Unconsciously across a noble brow,
And honor crowned a proud and lofty soul
With more of worth than human words allow.

How oft when brightest beams the morning sun,
Obscured the noonday lustre may appear ;

How oft persuasive eloquence is dumb

    To quell the passions—check the falling tear.

Aye, there are seasons when a demon power

    Controls the actions of the strongest mind,

Shrouds in perpetual gloom the passing hour,

    To pity deaf—to noble instinct blind.

Then comes the deep remorse which follows sin,

    Closed is each avenue of pure content ;

Wrecked all the glowing hopes that might have
      been,

    And every moment seems but idly spent.

While thus diverted by impassioned thought,

    The youthful maiden rose with measured gait,

And at the open casement trusting sought,

    To trace upon the Heavens her future fate.

She gazed ; a dark portentous cloud concealed

    From human view the glorious orb of night,

Beyond a deep reflection clear revealed

The silver lining to her tear–dimmed sight.

Quick as the flash of meteor, latent hope

Revived, "thank God! my heavy heart is gay,"

"The long dark night of sad despair," she spoke,

"Will be succeeded by perpetual day!"

PRESS FORWARD.

RESPECTFULLY INSCRIBED TO ABRAHAM LINCOLN,
MARCH 9TH, 1864.

PRESS forward! honored Chieftian of the land,

The nation's proudest hopes abide in thee,

Firm and unyielding still sublimely stand

God's instrument to perfect destiny.

But one bold stroke—one word divinely given,

Renders immortal thy unspotted name,

Revered on earth and doubly blessed by heaven,

The crisis–hour, and shall we ask in vain ?

Press forward! legions follow in thy rear,

· Devoted patriots to a righteous cause,

With holy purpose ever broad and clear—

The maintenance of duty's sacred laws.

77

Mark thou a policy so well defined
In simple words that never can decay,
While all the powers of evil yet combined
Will fail to cloud the straight unbroken way.

Press forward! mandates never premature,
Uttered by him who holds the needed power,
Make perfect right and justice more secure,
And hasten on the conflict's final hour.

Speak but one word—one firm but just command;
A proclamation in Jehovah's name,
The power that will redeem our native land—
Withhold it—the Republic dies in shame.

Press forward! time sufficient yet remains,
For Progress has unbounded faith in thee;
While loyalty wherever found exclaims,
"The Republic's true deliverer thou wilt be."

Give to the nation all the age requires,

A master–stroke of wisdom at thy hands,

Words whose grave import patriotism inspires,

And challenges the faith of foreign lands.

Press forward! Congress falters in the Right,

Then trust not in the legislative power;

But, Heaven sustained, remove the cause of strife,

The time for action now—the trial hour.

Let Freedom's flag be truthfully unfurled!

Break every chain that clouds the perfect day,

Do this—thou stands't the idol of the world,

The Alexander of America!

TO MY FATHER.

MY Father, oh, my Father!

While the flame of memory burns,

To the scenes of early childhood,

Wayward fancy gladly turns.

Days that passed in quick succession,

Bright and buoyant, gay and free,

Through the distant, buried seasons,

Every pulse beats true to thee.

My Father, oh, my Father!

Fancy wove a golden chain,

Linked together richer garlands

Than the monarch dares to claim.

Day–built visions rose before me,

Easy seemed life's flowing tide,

Deep eclipsed each ray of sorrow—
Every joy was magnified.

My Father, oh, my Father!
Not alone o'er marshy lea
Fanned by myriad tropic breezes
Did I wander drearily.
But thy gentle presence, Father,
Taught my youthful feet to stray
Fearlessly o'er verdant herbage,
Through the straight and certain way.

My Father, oh, my Father!
Not in vain thy fostering care,
As thy daughter's raven tresses
Floated in the silent air.
We have gone where rays of sunshine
Kiss the briny ocean's breast,
Viewed together golden landscapes
Sinking in the distant West.

My Father, oh, my Father !

Floats the mountain air the same,

And the lark, the morning singer,

Chaunts anew his sweet refrain.

Yet, alas ! deep, sad forebodings

Cloud the spirit's sweet repose,

Hours of silent contemplation

Sacred memories disclose.

My Father, oh, my Father !

When disease his mantle threw

O'er thy form—sad, sad the picture

My excited fancy drew.

Can it be ? Sweet Heaven, in mercy

Let the flush of health return,

Crown that brow with fresher chaplets—

Bid the vital spark to burn.

My Father, oh, my Father !

When earth's joys are dim to thee,

Leafy woods and budding flowers
  Lose their brightness then to me.
Yet my heart is wisely hoping,
  For a holy faith is mine,
That the stars now dimmed in glory,
  Shall in truer grandeur shine.

My Father, oh, my Father!
  All the laurels I may win,
Crown a brow whose richest blessings,
  From thy gentle counsel spring.
Oh, may some mysterious power
  Turn the shaft of destiny,
Lift the sombre veil of sadness—
  Heaven grant this boon to me!

ABSENT FRIENDS.

THE landscape tinted with celestial dye
Has faded with the sun's expiring ray,
While lengthened shadows gathering 'neath the sky,
Denote the close of day.

Time of sweet converse—season of repose,
When arduous labors with the eve expire,
While nature rests secure from mortal foes
I tune my feeble lyre.

Strung not by hand of art, my simple lay
Is but the measure of divided thought ;
I sing of those who tread the thorny way,
The southern clime have sought.

For with exalted purpose, teeming far

Beyond the narrow boundaries of life,

Shining with brilliance as the evening star,

They joined the mortal strife.

Three brothers in the pride of manhood's hour,

Vigorous and buoyant, with the glow of youth,

Launched their barks against despotic power,

Nobly to strike for truth.

Home, with the fond endearments clustering near,

Freighted with all the joy that love may claim,

Fails to allure when burns with• fervor clear,

The subtle, inward flame.

For patriotism knows not of that despair

Which forms the barrier to progression's tide,

But upward, onward, noble spirits dare,

Frail hopes are magnified.

One roams on Fernandina's hapless strand,

A glittering jewel in the diadems

Offered upon the altar of the land—

One of earth's priceless gems.

Two others near Potomac's wave-washed shore,

All sensual delights they freely give ;

Wealth. talent, all that manhood has in store,

That loyalty may live.

Gone forth unspotted, in God's fairy train,

Gone forth to struggle, manfully and brave,

That loss of life and treasure yet may gain

Freedom for every slave !

Oh ! may some guardian angel, hovering 'round

The scene of carnage, bid the storm abate ;

May spectral hands, in mystery profound,

Ward off the blow of fate !

May the strong hand of Omnipresent power
   Shiver to atoms all the cause of war,
To home and friends, tho' clouds still darkly lower,
   The absent yet restore!

THOUGHTS BESIDE THE SEA.

A WAY! enchanting memories of the past,

That fill. the measure of the thoughtless throng,

Rest for a season ere the winter blast

Brings with its advent gayer scenes along.

Let nature revelling in pure delight,

Exalt the soul to higher deeds of right.

How every impulse of the human heart

Bows in submission to Divine appeal,

When sober reason forms the counterpart

Of truth—the ideal blended with the real.

With reverence, Holy Father, unto Thee,

I muse in happy thought beside the sea.

88

Above, the firmament of azure hue,

   Below, foam—crested billows ceaseless roll,

Majestic! grand! as far as human view

   Extends, sublimity enshrouds the soul!

The orb of day reflects his glorious beams,

From briny surf a holy beauty gleams.

Far in the distance—o'er the wide expanse,

   Floats with the breeze the vessel's bleaching

     • sail ;

Around her smaller satellites advance,

   Bidding defiance to the sea—born gale.

Regardless whether friendly wind or tide,

She plows the deep in all her conscious pride.

Ah! who may know, though cloudless sets the sun,

   What unseen dangers she may yet endure ;

God grant propitious breezes waft her on

   To foreign climes protected and secure.

Success attend the mariner so brave,

And golden laurels thine beyond the grave!

While bright–eyed fancy hovers o'er the scene,

   And paints the unfading glory of the hour,

The evening shadows gather 'round serene,

   And star–gemmed night asserts her wonted

     power,

In awful grandeur still the billows roll,

Eternal harmony pervades the whole!

Come forth! oh Athiest, on the wave–washed

     strand,

   And view the mighty wonders of the sea;

Then dare assert less than Almighty hand,

   Controls the tempest—rules thy destiny!

Strike off the fetters to a blind belief,

And thus afford thy better thoughts relief.

If thou can'st stand a living witness here,

To God's creative wisdom, and be blind,—

Sad, sad the thought a heart so dumb and sear,

And lost to truth with such a poisoned mind,

Oh, Great Jehovah! these the base, untrue,

" Forgive them, for they know not what they do!"

Aye, thus the dazzling splendor of the main,

Thrills through the deepest recess of the soul,

Inspiring homage for Jehovah's name.

Through countless ages dark blue oceans roll !

Charmed by thy potent power, oh, rolling sea,

Life is sublime alone with God and thee !

THE STATUE OF FREEDOM.

"We have placed over the edifice in which our laws are to be enacted the effigy of Freedom. We have put it there in token of our acknowledgment that, in the sight of Justice, no man is born a Master, and no man is born a Slave!"—*Tribune.*

UPON thy dome, proud temple of the State!

Moulding with wisdom the decrees of fate,

Through the vast space of ether safely borne,

Freedom's Colossus rears her bronzed form.

While with supremest power her silver wand

Brings peace and plenty to a foreign land;

Unites again ties of fraternal love,

Springing spontaneous from the founts above!

Proud monument of truth and moral worth!

We hail with joy the Nation's Christian ·birth.

Ages of darkness 'neath thy power fade,

As leaves of Autumn lose their verdant shade.

The fiery missles despotism hurled,

Stand twice condemned before a generous world.

Two revolutions sweep the surface clear,

And Freedom triumphs o'er the silent bier!

Before thy shrine the guiltless humbly bow,

Millions of sable worshippers hast thou!

Ideal aspirations now are real,

Though yet unsheathed remains the glittering steel.

For with thy noble image beckoning on,

Beneath the glitter of the noon-day sun,

The throes of agony which shake the world,

Will be to dark oblivion fiercely hurled.

Colossal Statue! no frail spirits moan

In suppliant accents at thy polished throne.

No dark skinned mother trembling with despair,

Sees borne from sight her infant bright and fair.

No youthful quadroon supplicates in vain
That bartered charms may be her own again.
No sable brother with uplifted eyes,
Frantic with misery, curses man and dies.

For from the fertile valleys of the North,
The sun of Freedom brilliantly beams forth,
Reflected by the statue wisdom rears
O'er Southern pines to quell the captive's fears.
Vermillion–dyed the stream of conflict flows,
Man reaps the whirlwind when he blindly sows ;
Yet stands the form of Liberty sublime,
Just representative of truth divine.

While England's taunt she sent across the wave,
" America's no refuge for the slave !"
From whence it came we hurl defiantly,
And mock her for the basest treachery.
Aye, once again the soil the Pilgrims trod,
Is consecrated by the hand of God !
Artistic skill in lands beyond the sea,
Goddess of Freedom is eclipsed by thee !

THE LANDSCAPE.

WOOED beyond life's troubled waters,
  By a strange mysterious power,
Deep unfathomed thought in silence,
  Traces what enchants the hour.
Distant far the glowing sunset
  Holds the thoughts with spell divine,
To increase the magic splendor,
  All the rainbow tints combine.

See! now bright and still more brightly
  Orange–tinted clouds appear,
Clothing all the pure horizon
  With a beauty soft and clear.
Peacefully the hills and valleys
  Still their verdant robes retain,

Save where in exalted contrast,

Waves o'er–ripe the golden grain,

.

Through the meadow rich in herbage,

Glides the rippling stream away,

Mirrored on its glassy surface,

Bush and tree reflected lay.

Song of birds—the swallows twittering

'Round the prickly hedge of thorn,

Through all animated nature,

Flows the life–blood rich and warm.

Yet again the eye delighted,

Scans a field of growing maize,

Picturing scenes of busy labor,

In the future autumn days.

Flowers, incense–breathing flowers,

With the cooing of the dove—

Gifted nature's choicest blessings,

Heaven's messengers of love !

Look beyond yon circling cedars!
  Moves the lowing herd along,
Urged by instinct true and earnest,
  By a purpose firm and strong.
Once again the dewy clover
  Yields beneath their steady feet,
Once again the twilight shadows
  Gather 'round my lone retreat.

Homeward bound the weary reaper
  Feels a secret sense of joy,
As he notes his gathered treasures—
  Peace, sweet peace, without alloy.
Thine is rest to wealth unknown,
  Thine is pleasure's earnest thrill,
Filling up the greatest measure
  Of our Heavenly Father's will.

Through the floating waves of ether,
  Redolent with summer blooms,
Fade the deeper tints of sunset,
  'Neath the shroud that night assumes.

Aye, the world may boast of wisdom,
  In her stately halls of pride,
But the holiest founts of feeling,
  There remain ungratified.

Would ye know the deep impressions
  That creative power reveals?
Go to where enchanting nature,
  Bitter scenes of life conceals.
Talent brightens when enraptured,
  As the human pulses beat,
When upon life's troubled surface,
  Hearts congenial chance to meet.

There are secret wells of feeling,
  Secret throbs of joy and pain,
That impassioned thought endeavors
  To control, but all in vain.
There are scenes of happy romance,
  Making bright this changeful clime,
In the far out-stretching landscape,
  Great Jehovah! all are Thine!

REDEEMED: JANUARY 31 ST, 1865.

STAND forth brave nation, cleansed and
purified,
Upon thy soil to consecration given
Flows on in grandeur the exhaustless tide
Of Progress, 'neath the sweetest smiles of
Heaven.

Divinely shaped thy destiny unfolds,
Redeemed when in the zenith of thy fame!
As unseen power the future wisely moulds,
Through war and carnage breaks the captive's
chain.

Aye! not in rain the crimson tide has flowed,
Or brightest hopes been wrecked upon the
strand,

The choicest blessing Heaven has e'er bestowed,

Now stands pre-eminent—sublimely grand.

The loyal heart beats strong and firm to-day,

With renewed courage joins the mortal strife,

While truth and justice chase the clouds away,

The captive falters, thanks to Heaven, for life!

Ye honored few! who, reared in Southern climes

Amid oppression's pestilential power,

Raised your right hands to crush the nation's

crimes,

Are doubly blessed in this our trial-hour.

No eulogy those noble names require,

Whose voices heard in Legislative halls,

Were actuated by the grand desire

To follow when the voice of duty calls.

Immortalized the scroll of honor stands!

A mausoleum Time can ne'er efface,

A solid column formed by loyal hands,

Upon whose record stands no bitter trace.

Soon will oblivion bury in the past,

The time-worn relics despotism formed,

And Freedom reign triumphantly at last,

Above the citadel oppression stormed!

Soon boasted chivalry will fade away

As Autumn leaves 'neath winter's chilly breath,

Exultingly we hail the glorious day,

Of Freedom's birth and stern oppression's death!

For brighter skies and calmer seas of strife,

For this the greatest, grandest victory,

And conquests bold that saved the nation's life,

Though dearly bought, Jehovah! thanks to Thee!

THE SPIRIT OF WINTER.

SHRILL winds wail o'er the barren hills.
　　The spirit of winter is brave,
Silent the voice of the ice–bound rills,
　　That a clearer passage crave.
Mute the warblings of many birds,
　　Absent their musical strains,
Housed from tempest the grazing herds—
　　Through the wood float wild refrains.

Icy the breath of the passing breeze,
　　On the frosted window pane,
Swayed by the storm, the leafless trees
　　Bend their proud forms in disdain.
Leaf–tongues are silent, but louder notes
　　Swell with the gathering storm,

Mandates of Summer, Winter revokes,
   Leaving her domain forlorn.

Soon the pure white snow–flakes appear,
   Robing with ermine the earth,
Scenes of sorrow fade on their bier,
   Leaving but sunshine and mirth;
Shadows of evening gather 'round,
   Pure is the current of delight,
Filled is the air with musical sound,
   Charmed is the sensual sight.

Ye, who would blight the joys of youth,
   'Neath religion's mistaken vow,
Voices of nature will teach the truth,
   As to her ye humbly bow.
Then let the voices of childhood raise
   To God their anthems of love,
Beneath the snow, with notes of praise!
   And the azure sky above!

Thou who assumeth the saintly shroud,
   And walketh from the world apart,

13

With saintly look and bearing proud,

God does not dwell in thy heart!

But take the child—the maiden fair,

Or age with the chastening rod,

Where truth prevails the silver hair

Reveals the image of God!

But once again divided thought

Resumes the rested lyre of praise,

Oh! scenes of winter gaily sought,

Too rapid the fleeting days.

Yon forest trees that bravely grow,

With verdant foliage waved,

Now bend beneath the virgin snow,

And bless the hand that saved!

Prismatic colors of rainbow dye,

The clearness of sunlight reveal,

The spangled boughs—the azure sky—

The bliss of Heaven conceal.

Forces of nature strangely blend,
  To brighten the pathway of life,
While all the works of Creation lend
  True rays of wisdom and light!

Hail! ye winds, ye clouds, and ye storms!
  Ye vapors so heavy and grim!
Emblems of Winter—spirit forms,
  Exalting the soul to Him!
But from the destitute, mournful tones,
  Seasons of misery untold,
Many weep as the North wind moans,
  Sigh, "I am cold, oh! so cold!"

Father of all! from thy Throne of Grace!
  Shield the deserted and sad,
Scatter thy blessings—sorrow erase,
  Make their hearts peaceful and glad!
Spirit of Winter! thanks to thee,
  For leading us nearer to God,
May thy revealings ever be free,
  'Till we rest beneath the sod!

THE BIRTH-DAY OF LIBERTY.

DAY dawns: the darkened shades of night
    have fled,
While tranquil nature hushed o'er land and sea,
    Awakes with murmured blessing o'er the dead,
    And whispers soft the magic words—"Be Free!"

The southern pines take up the joyful strain,
    And waft their greeting to an injured race,
While o'er the lofty granite hills of Maine,
    The New Year wears a bright and smiling face.

Aye, every heart where Truth and Right prevail,
    Beats warm and high on Freedom's natal day,
And every voice however weak and frail,
    In trembling accents joins the cheerful lay.

The tyrant's rod has lost its fatal power,

    The boon of Freedom God in justice gave,

The ruling feeling of the day and hour

    Like perfumed zephyrs, floats above the slave!

No more our dusky brothers toil in vain,

    But every thought to noble purpose given,

The joyful cadence of their wild refrain,

    Ascends with praise the peaceful dome of

    Heaven.

Then bless the man who raised his voice on high,

    In firm obedience to Divine appeal,

Who with a purpose crowned the battle-cry!

    And stern, unyielding, broke oppression's seal!

Aye, haughty Southron, bold, defiant still,

    The chains of death by iron hands are riven,

While Justice claims with an undaunted will,

    This day to holy consecration given!

Ye Poets! who in fantasy abide,

Invoke the Muses to inspired zeal,

And let your influence swell the common tide,

Until to Justice human beings kneel!

Ye gifted Authors! tune your lyres anew,

And be not loitering in the hour of need,

The friends of human progress look to you,

For words of cheer, an earnest, firm, "God
speed!"

We mourn as only hearts afflicted, mourn,

O'er those who float upon a crimson sea,

But Justice firmly answers through the storm,

"Cease not till every human soul is free!"

It comes! the bright millenium o'er the earth,

Not distant far when sin and sorrow cease,

Then hail! all hail! the day of Freedom's birth,

The glorious harbinger of lasting peace!

IN MEMORY OF ABRAHAM LINCOLN.

"THUS HATH THE RIGHTEOUS FALLEN!"

OH weep, Columbia! weep in anguish deep,
  Weep tears of blood above a martyr's grave,
Sound the sad requiem—midnight vigils keep,
  In deepest mourning let our Banner wave!

The deadening pressure of this trial hour,
  The words of agony on breezes borne,
The loss, oh hero, of thy conscious power,
  Has left the nation sad, bereft, forlorn.

The senses reel beneath this stunning blow,
  Extinguished seems the glorious light of day,
Exultant triumphs o'er a vanquished foe,
  Are dead to thought—and glory fades away.

The nation's heart with feeble pulses beats,

　And dumb with sorrow now prostrated lies,

Thy welcome voice no more our victories greets,

　Deep lamentations on the air arise.

We do not mourn thy advent to that sphere,

　Where life eternal blesses such as thou,

But, oh! we sadly miss thy presence here—

　Yet to Divine permission humbly bow.

Historic page will glitter with thy name,

　Though dimly now shines Freedom's radiant sun,

For though thy mortal life we cannot claim,

　Champion of Right! thy soul is marching on!

With bonds of steel thy blood cements this land,

　Freedom's sure triumph with thy latest breath,

Grief bids defiance to the coward hand,

　Who dared to wield the instrument of death!

Come Retribution! come, in all thy power,

   Annihilating with the tyrant's rod,

Revenge and death! the watchword of the hour—

   And leave the rest to Justice and to God.

Oh, Great Jehovah! humbly do we kneel,

   And supplicate before Thy righteous Throne,

For blighted hopes and prospects thou canst heal—

   We cannot tread the thorny way alone.

Oh, Great Preserver! guide the ship aright!

   Our faithful helmsman sleeps in death's embrace,

In deep humility we pray for light,

   And trust repose upon Thy pardoning grace.

Rest, modest hero! rest in peace profound!

   Free from the scenes of strife this world of sin—

We seem to hear the ever welcome sound:

   "Well done, and faithful servant, enter in!"

14

THE HOUSEHOLD.

A MONG the emerald hills in rustic ease,

The homestead stands, within the maple shade
The songster tunes his joyful lay to please
Dame nature in her grandest style arrayed.

Without is all enchantment and repose,

The soul's ideal of eternal rest,
The beautiful in fairest type compose

A rural scene by highest power blest.

Beyond the threshold active forms appear,

Congenial with God's approved design,
Filling the measure in this lower sphere,

Of human worth, where faith and hope combine·

One, the dear Father of the household band,

A man of books, from all the world apart

Save from the pure, home–circle ; his command

Comes from the promptings of an earnest heart.

Silence his watchword ! yet with speaking eyes,

That glow with untold worth—a world of thought

Concealed from human view, his soul denies

The truth of much the sorrow life has wrought.

Too unbelieving, too gentle for a man,

Presuming not enough to make the way

Of life easy and sure ; the social ban

Thus understood dims the light of day.

A worshipper at nature's shrine, the stars

Beam through his vision with a purer light,

Nothing around, above, below that mars

The perfect form of scientific sight.

Learned yet unlearned, knowing of treasured love

Contained upon the printed page, yet blind

To human frailty—and believing more

In words than actions as regards mankind.

His partner through the ills that may betide,

A worthy woman fills her perfect sphere ;

A dear, loved Mother sits the board beside,

And lends her presence to the sweet home-cheer.

First, when the voice of duty prompts the way,

Benevolent in all her thoughts and deeds,

Cheering the prospects of the darkest day—

Foremost in all life's duties and life's needs.

Help to the poor her generous hand extends;

Quick of perception, in expression free,

Candor with pure intentions grandly blends

And forms the basis of maturity.

Long ere the public mind was near prepared
To plead the cause of liberty and right,
Her heart the misery of the captive shared,
And ached to view the nation's blinded sight.

O genial soul! though streaks of grey are seen
To mingle with the darkly shaded hair,
May life prolonged be ever bright and green,
A foretaste of that world the good may share.

Next a fond daughter on the scene appears,
The harbinger that God vouchsafed to send
To cheer the pathway of declining years,
And to the present added comfort lend.

Something of talent beams upon her brow,
Enough to gladden life's appointed way—
Enough a higher nature to endow,
And to her spirit better thoughts convey.

Astray her youthful feet how oft are led
  By impulses perhaps too quick obeyed;
An earnest nature—and if rightly read
  The critic finds his censure oft delayed.

One whose convictions seem to lead her on
  Beyond the standard public thought approved—
A moralist whose highest hopes are won,
  When evil through conviction is removed.

Another form uniting strength of hope,
  Firmness of purpose and devotion true,
A nature grasping for a wider scope—
  Completes the picture memory brings to view.

Light of the household, what a treasure there!
  A happy being moves the world among;
Age, adverse fortune will not cause despair,
  Vivacious thought will make her always young.

How laughter-loving does her face appear

    A God-send to the heart in mental strife,

So much of vital force the world to cheer,

    Enjoying every particle of life.

Oft times, when summer zephyrs soft and pure,

    Invite the wanderer from the city's din,

From stifled air the feeble frame allure,

    Back to its home the vital current win.;

'Tis then a gentle Aunt may linger near,

    Companion in the household's busy scene—

Loveliest of the lovely, ever dear,

    Angelical in spirit, true, serene.

How much of all that honest merit claims,

    Is stamped upon·the brow of human worth,

How much mature and peaceful age retains

    Of youth's bright promise—of celestial birth.

O, noble heart ! may Heaven guide thee on,

  With garlands crown the path of life serene,

Until the bright and blissful shore is won,

  Thy sun of promise sets in peace supreme!

Such is the household ;—'tis no fancy view ;

  Distinctly marked the page of memory,—

They move, they breathe, the heart's impulses true,

  These human beings, 'midst infinity.

RETROSPECTION.

SILENTLY, on unseen pinions,
    Thought a higher standard gains,
Linking bright or sad emotions,
    Fancy weaves her perfect chains.
Backward, past the buried seasons,
    Through the dim, uncertain light
View we now the nation's trials,
    Moments dark as endless night.

Time was when with fear and trembling
    Stood our dear, beloved land,
On the verge of certain ruin,
    Crushed beneath the tyrant's hand.
Weeks and months the deep vibrations
    Of the cannon's fearful sound,

Spoke in unmistaken accents,

Pointed to the battle ground.

As those hopes so blindly cherished

By defeat began to wane,

'Round his limbs the rude oppressor

Closer drew the captive's chain.

Patriot zeal in Southern dungeons,

Blighted by starvation's power,

Brutish force alone created

All the misery of that hour.

But in vain : our sainted ruler

Struck the motive power of Right !

Raising from those swarthy heroes,

Noble allies for the strife.

Time passed on : four years of anguish—

'Tis the oft repeated tale,

Broken households—widows mourning

Mingled wtih the orphan's wail.

But at last the clouds divided

   And the glorious sunlight came;

Rest for all, the promise given,

   To the slave a broken chain.

Was this all? Did treason slumber

   After rounds of sad defeat?

Yielding up in silent wisdom

   To the conqueror's steady beat?

No! not so; oh sickening vision,

   See a nation blind with tears,

Strong men bowed as if declining

   'Neath the sudden weight of years.

Dimmed the stars on Freedom's banner,

   When the dreadful tidings burst

On the air, " Our Chief has fallen!"

   Treason did indeed its worst.

But enough. The heart is saddened

   By this weary waste of years;

Gladly draw we close the curtain

That conceals abiding fears.

Once again the wheels of power,

Re-anointed work anew,

Sending forth fraternal greeting

To the truly loyal few.

Warrior, rest! thy crown of glory,

Is with brightest jewels set,

Sheathe the sword in trust forever—

Bravely hast thou paid thy debt.

Thanks to God! perpetual freedom

Brings to all a sweet release,

Thanks to God! the nation liveth

Blessed with a perpetual Peace!

SUNSET IN AUTUMN.

UNFOLDS the landscape to the gazer's view,

The Sun's declining rays dim shadows cast,

Rich with autumnal tints of varied hue,

Nature repeats the changes of the past.

Behold! yon forest dipped in choicest dye,

Garnet and gold in rich profusion blent,

Reflected by the splendor of the sky,

In bold relief upon the firmament.

Pause: there is room for contemplation here,

With light and shade, sunshine and clouds combined,

With rainbow tints—the silence of the bier—

The elements in truest sense defined.

123

Look to the West! a cloud obscures the sun
But for one moment—bursting forth in flame,
Illuming earth and heaven—the portal won
That opes to human sight celestial gain.

Streaks of bright crimson, waves of burnished gold,
Ridge above ridge of many shades of dye,
With orange-tinted cloud fold upon fold,
Appear upon the western waste of sky.

Beholding this, glance to the distant scene,
Magnificent with colored autumn leaves,
Intensified by rays of sunlight gleam,
On the rapt sight the stately forest trees.

Painter of Athens! bring your easel here,
Spread the broad canvas! inspiration true
Will make the line of beauty bold and clear
To blunted vision—and fair fame for you.

None, there are none can paint a scene like this,

'Tis far beyond the claim of gifted man,

The harbinger of that Eternal bliss,

Soul–satisfying, that the few may scan.

Ye! who unmindful of the passing view,

Deem ye this but a flight of fancy? Go

With thought unbiased, mark with motive true, ;

Autuminal change—the sunset's ruddy glow.

So much of light divine, of hope and joy

Is mirrored on the calm, clear azure sky,

So much of Heaven is stamped without alloy

On nature's brow, to prove the skeptic's lie.

Sinks in the West the glorious orb of day!

Fadeth from view the clear and tranquil sight,

While gently o'er kind nature's grand display,

In peace supreme descend the shades of night!

HAIL! Heaven–born heritage of Right!
Developed with life's earliest breath,
For love of thee brave millions dare
To cross the boundary line of death.
For love of thee the human heart
Impassioned, pulsates deep and strong,
And every life–strung nerve secure,
With firmer tension combats wrong.

For thee, the patient captive waits,
And breathes his last sigh on the air,
For thee, the bond–mother dares to take
The life of innocence so fair,
And as she notes the parting breath
Of her sweet babe from bondage free,

One prayer to God—her sacrifice

Upon thy throne, O Liberty!

Columbus tracked the ocean's waste,

And landed on the wave–washed shore,

The ebbing tide of hope returned,

And all the air a freshness bore.

Still later in the tide of years,

The Mayflower crossed the surging sea—

Jehovah clothed with potency,

These harbingers of Liberty.

Anon the landscape dotted o'er

With scenes that thrilled the anxious sight,

While Justice dared to wield the rod,

And touch the mystic spring of Right!

Brave, stalwart frames with voice and arm,

Responsive rose in freedom's line,

Oppression paused—recoiled before

The dawn of Liberty divine!

16

Almost a century of light

  And shade has passed away ; this hour

The Orient light of early morn

  Is dimmed by treachery's power.

Although the landscape lies before,

  Arrayed with every purpose grand,

With scarce a trace of buried worth

  To mark a free and rescued land.

Night in America ! four years

Of darkness and of anguish borne,

Until a master–spirit broke

  The captive's chains and quelled the storm.

From southern pines rose shouts of joy,

  That thrilled the main from sea to sea—

From dark, impending clouds broke forth

  The brilliant rays of Liberty !

Light on the beacon–land ! afar

  Is mirrored on the azure sky,

The alien reaches forth his hands,

  And bids his native home good-bye!

He braves the dangers of the deep,

  To die upon the stormy wave,

Rather than bear oppression's wrongs,

  And live to be an Emperor's slave!

Great Garibaldi silent weeps—

  But who can fathom massive thought?

Though vanquished now, what deep designs,

  In silent wisdom may be wrought?

Fair Italy! though slumbering now

  Beneath an imbecile's rude sway,

The light will come—thy promised hopes

  Shall bloom on Freedom's natal day!

Crush if you will the budding flower,

  But still the root unbidden lives,

And ere the watchful eye desires

  Springs forth and richer fragrance gives.

Away, beyond the ocean's tide,

Exultant floated from afar

Sweet strains of Liberty and Peace,

While millions bless the Russian Czar!

Thus are the elements of Right

Triumphant even unto death ;

Thus in progression's steady march,

You cannot stifle Freedom's breath !

For manhood scorns the proffered aid

Of treachery, and dares to do,

Though compassed 'round with adverse fate,

All that is generous, just and true.

Check if you will the current strong

That sweeps humanity's broad tide,

By recreant votes in Senate Halls,

Forget the cause death sanctified ;

Spread if you will the world afar,

The emblems of despotic zeal,

And from the man that power makes slave,

   All his just rights in triumph steal ;—

Still will the flame of Justice burn,

   Still will the soul, uplifted high,

Drink from the treasures mirrored there

   And the base tyrant's threats defy.

Still will the flag of Freedom wave!

   In all its potent power unfurled,

Blessing with every purpose free,

   One God, one Nation, and one World!

THE VETO.

Written after the veto of the Civil Rights Bill by
President Johnson, 1866.

'TIS done! the cruel deed of shame is done!

And will the nation yield in mute despair

To one weak man? with half the conquest won

While tones of anguish fill the trembling air?

Will justice slumber 'neath the burden laid

By coward hands on Progress far and wide?

And will our noble patriots thus betrayed

Yield in submission to the weaker side?

Will Congress paralyzed withhold her right

To act, despite the heavy weight of power?

132

And self–sustaining lift the cloud of night
   Which hovers o'er the duties of the hour?

Are all the sighs, the groans, the bitter tears,
   The smothered accents of a grief sublime,
The blood–stained record of the last four years,
   But naught to expiate the nation's crime?

Shall all the prayers ascending to Thy throne,
   From that dejected and unfortunate race
Reap no reward? but must they walk alone,
   With nothing in the future bright to trace?

It cannot be : the balm of every age,
   That all sustaining faith in God and Right,
Buoys up the soul of patriot and sage,
   Dispells the darkness that obscures the light!

Oh! sainted Lincoln! to all races true,
   Well may our sable brethern mourn in vain,

When all was bright—the promised day in view,
Those sad eyes closed—and all was dark again.

                              .

Oh! burdened race! where is your Moses now?
On whom may ye your earnest trust bestow?
Not to the nation's Ruler need ye bow,
He who should lead is freedom's treacherous foe!

Then freemen! rally to the work once more
In Congress still the world may proudly trust,
And though conflicting tides we may deplore,
An unseen power whispers, "God is just!"

THE REAPERS.

CALM and lovely lies the landscape
  'Neath the glorious summer sun,
Hope and joy with light and gladness,
  Blend harmonious into one.
All the air with incense laden,
  Wafts the breath of new-mown. hay,
Until dews of evening gather,
  Until night succeeds the day.

Early dawn allures the reaper
  From his easy couch of rest,
With inviting smiles of nature—
  Labor that is truly blest.
Happy in the thought, that gathered
  Ere to-morrow's setting sun,

All the products of the season,

Will by toil be richly won.

Look beyond yon marshy meadow,

Still beyond the forest trees,

See ! the golden grain is waving

To the sighing of the breeze.

O'er the hills a happy trio

Move their steady pace along,

To the quiet thrill of pleasure,

To the reaper's triumph song.

As their stalwart forms are bending

O'er the golden–headed grain,

Manhood reaps a proud addition

To the knowledge he may gain.

Soon the proudly waving acres,

God's high mandate thus obeyed,

One by one now lie prostrated,

Yielding to the whetted blade.

There is music on the waters,

There is music on the land,

Joy upon the trackless ocean,

Pleasure on the wave–washed strand.

But the sweetest note of music

Is the sickle's accolade,

And the highest scene of transport,

That which honest toil has made.

High above the clear horizon,

Casts the sun his scorching beams,

In the zenith of his power,

Heaven's brightness through him gleams.

Hark! away, away in distance,

Sounds the gong's repeated beat.

And the harvesters exulting

Find but half their task complete.

Homeward, to a home made lovely

By the daughters of the soil,

Choicest food for him who hungers,

Rest from heat and daily toil.

Pure and clear the crystal water,

Quaffed by thirsty lips the while,

Free from alcoholic poison,

Blessed by Heaven's grateful smile !

But not long the reapers tarry,

Soon their temporal wants supplied,

When again the grain–field labor

They resume with conscious pride.

Now the sheaves are being gathered,

Now the trusty team in view,

Busy hands complete the labor,

Bolder efforts now renew.

Soon the last sheaf upward lifted,

Shouts of triumph on the breeze,

Echo from the distant mountain,

And re–echo through the trees.

Home again! oh, joyous moments,
  Freighted with celestial bloom,
Home again! the Eternal reaper,
  Scarce can call the good too soon.

Calm and lovely lies the landscape
  'Neath the glorious setting sun,
Day departing, unseen spirits
  Whisper softly, "bravely done!"
Blessed by God in every treasure,
  Thankful for this sweet release,
Deep in thought and high in purpose,
  Rest! ye harvesters, in peace!

A SABBATH MEMORY.

ALL the air is richly laden with the fragrant
breath of Spring,
Tones harmonious sweetly blending through earth's
joyous portals ring.
Bearing thus a strong resemblance to that mournful Sabbath morn,
When into promised heaven was a master–spirit
born.

Full twelve months of light and shadow have
their annual circle run,
Full twelve months since treason vanquished freedom's era was begun.
As the stormy waves of conflict still receded
from the shore,

Brightly glowed the pure horizon that was clouded
o'er before.

Richmond fallen! oh, what visions of a blissful
future rise,
Truth triumphant, swell the chorus 'neath the
blue and arching skies.
Could we paint a purer picture : leading childhood
by the hand,
Thus into the conquered City walked the Moses
of our land!

Youth and age, untutored manhood one spontaneous homage gave
To the master–mind who meekly, heaven–directed
came to save.
Happy seemed the dark assemblage " touching
but his garment's hem,"
Came from thousands thus delivered in response
the deep " Amen ! "

Sabbath   dawns.   What   strange   transition   wraps
        the   continent   in   gloom,
Did   the   blooms   of   early   spring–time   premature
        advance   too   soon ?
Sabbath   dawns.   Why   all   this   mourning,   plaintive
        sobs   and   stifled   moan,
Has   some   fearful   epidemic   stricken   one   from
        every   home ?

Let   the   mourning   millions   answer,   for   poetic
        efforts   fail
Calmly   to   portray   the   sorrow   or   rehearse   the
        burdened   tale.
Time   may   soothe   the   aching   spirit,   but   it   never
        can   efface,
What   has   been   the   saddest   record   that   historic
        pen   can   trace.

One   has   gained   Eternal   glory—one   now   fills   the
        vacant   chair,

To the first a nation's homage—to the last a
nation's care.

Twice condemned, superior wisdom still to loyalty
is true,

Strike again thou modern Pharoah! it is all that
thou canst do.

Vividly does faithful memory freighted with a tale
of woe,

Picture in their onward progress what has darkened all below.

Lincoln dead! the choicest blessing snatched from
mortal diadem,

Earth has yielded up the treasure, Heaven holds
the priceless gem!

18

A LONE beside Niagara's swelling tide,

    Behold, the splendor of the Orient light

That ushers in the Sabbath morn! Beside

    This classic stream enraptured human sight

Through nature's revelations lifts the soul

Beyond external life to virtue's goal.

Upon this mighty flood do thousands gaze,

    Youth, age and childhood come but to revere

Jehovah's name ; the artist and the sage

    Renew their efforts to portray in clear

And fervid style ; 'tis the oft–told tale—

The pencil and acquired wisdom fail.

144

The muse of poetry may try her skill,

  As yet vacuity her task succeeds,

In each successive effort of the will,

  The grand phenomenon in triumph leads.

With all the worth that literature contains,

A vacuum in human words remains.

We need no dogmas here, enough to feel

  The present power of supreme decree

Enough to know as silently we kneel,

  God hears the appeal though mute the lips

      may be.

Oh ! the sweet solace of a secret prayer,

Firm in the faith that never can despair.

No chime of bells—no organ's melody

  Breaks the sweet, holy charm ; but grander far

Is the incessant roar of waters ; free

  From creeds that oppress, no superstitions mar

The Heavenly influence, but alone with God,

Do contrite spirits kiss the chastening rod !

No artist work of angels on the wing,

  No gilded ornament adorns the dome,

No golden cross, to which the few may cling

  With fear and trembling, call the sinner home.

Naught but the deep blue firmament above,

The sea of air, enduring as God's love.

Our faltering feet no velvet surface tread,

  Indicative of fashion, wealth and pride;

We bow the knee by custom's power led,

  To meet no cushioned seat—what then beside ?

Naught but a rock of ages stand we on,

And feel the truest way to Heaven is won !

Ye proselytes ! exacting in your creed,

  Who clothe Religion with a sombre shroud,

And fancy you discern what all may need

  To find God's presence, your exhortings loud

Fall on unheeding ears, for reason's light

Will guide the wanderer through the clouds of

    night.

Thus inconsistency is virtue's bane,

But, oh! Niagara, on this Sabbath morn,

We worship God through thee, yet make no claim

Superior to what is human born.

Our sacrament—the triumphs over sin,

'Tis thus we pledge our fealty to Him.

Majestic flood! in all thy power flow on,

Superior mandates in thy course fulfil,

The greatest wonder 'neath the glorious sun!

The grandest triumph of Almighty will!

We gaze entranced, and feel with thought sincere,

Freer from sin—nearer to Heaven when here.

THE AGE OF PROGRESS.

ONE century. In retrospective view

The vanished years return ; reflected light
Illumes the record ever brave and true

That demonstrates progressive thought and sight.
We move through space eternal as the sun,
Yet find the age of wisdom scarce begun.

Time was when dull, uneducated thought

Repelled the advance of Science and of Right,
The voice of Progress braver spirits sought,

To work unceasing in this world of light ;
That far and near the restless soul may find
An antidote—a shield for all mankind.

148

When Franklin drew the lightning from the sky'
  Men doubted, almost scorned the brave attempt,
As infidel to Him who rules on high—
  Thus for a season knowledge seemed content.
'Twas left for other hands to pave the way,
And lead from darkness to the perfect day!

It came ; the light of Science beamed anew!
  Quick to respond the field of thought was won,
When Morse revealed the inspiration true,
  And sent the electric current flashing on!
Amid the ceaseless tide of modern craft,
God bless the inventor of the Telegraph!

With new accessions to ambition's throne,
  The grand advance of art and science came ;
The eventful past abounds with deeds alone,
  Of thrilling import and of vital claim.
As years rolled on the aching vision traced
A glorious record not to be erased.

The mighty ocean at the summons lends
   Its potent influence to futurity,
As continent to continent extends
   Fraternal greeting 'neath the rolling sea.
Protected by superior skill beside,
The Atlantic Cable stems the seething tide!

When first a message passed beneath the wave,
   How reckless every thought of triumph seemed,
Devoid of that which doubting beings crave,
   No ray of sunshine through the darkness beamed,
But soon the race that leads to light was run—
Thus ignorance rebelled but knowledge won.

With all the triumphs Progress dared to claim,
   And all the efforts Science did display,
America concealed the deadly bane
   Of permanent renown, and lost the day.
How strange! when much was won that nation's
      seek,
This country in her proudest hour was weak.

Strange ! aye, perhaps it was to unskilled art, ·

   In things pertaining to the human will,

The earnest throbbings of the human heart

   For Justice, would not, dared not to be still.

Five years ago the war for freedom ceased,

And in response prosperity increased.

As slavery died, the incubus destroyed,

   That dimmed the lustre of our country's fame,

Upward the star of promise rose ! annoyed

   By no vile tempter to consume the gain.

But steadily it shone with added light,

Day follows and conceals the long, dark night.

Night :—with the bondman from the cruel foe,

   Concealed within malarious swamps to die ;

Night :—with the bondmother's frantic wail of woe,

   Nerving her spirit for the last " good bye !"

Night :—with the groaning of the wounded brave,

Denied the drink his dying thirst might crave.

19

Oh! there are visions of the past so clear
And yet so sad, we gladly turn the page
Of history to welcome better cheer,
That still excels in this progressive age.
Lo! how the forces of success unite
In worshipping before the throne of Right!

To-day the life-blood of the nation flows
In stronger current ; far across the land
Glad tidings come ; the artizan bestows
His measure of the work—the iron band :
Thus do we view with earnest hearts content,
The iron track across the continent.

Onward! flow onward, generous tide of years,
While man to greater wisdom may attain,
Gifted beyond conception ; talent rears
The promised goal of earthly hope and fame.
Onward! press onward, ye whose mental sight,
Eternal beams with Heaven's reflected light!

Hark! to the distant echoes; why despair,

  While contemplating all the world has won?

Hark! to the distant echoes: on the air

  Prophetic voices thus exulting come:

" Knowledge for all nations, Freedom's birthright!

Progression for oppression—day for night!"